Foreword

In the summer of 2015, I first made a few attempts at writing poetry. Previously I had written prose including drafts for novels and flash fiction. I found writing poetry to be cathartic in that things I had observed could be embellished into mini stories and mini situations. I could merge the characteristics or personalities of two or more people with the image of stock characters in order to create entertaining poems for a small circle of friends.

I wrote a few poems or small collection of poems specifically for individuals who I had respect for. Hopefully, they enjoyed what I wrote about them and took it with great humour.

Some of the poems I wrote for those people, and some which are totally fictitious, are in this collection, *Do you recognise yourself?* However, as stated, people and events are mainly either merged, distorted and embellished, or made up. For example, the poem 'Jenny' I could have named Debbie, Penny, Kelly, Demi, Emmy, Eddie, Teddy, Betty etc. I just had to decide on a name that rhymed. So no offence to anyone with the name 'Jenny' out there. In the words of Ant and Dec, "It's not you." Similarly poems such as 'Evil Man' and 'Evil Woman' are embellished to the extent that surely no one can be as evil as them. Surely such people only live in soap operas. On the other hand I have to admit that poems such as 'Words' and 'Guided' were written for specific people and they know who they are. Finally, there are poems which were written for specific people with their names in it, and again they know who they are and they have given permission for those poems to be included. (So they *do recognise themselves*.)

Although many of the poems are humorous, there are also some which are extreme and gritty. Unfortunately, in life such people and situations do exist and so I felt it was necessary to include such characters as well.

There are some poems that were too outrageous for this collection and they will be included in *The Banned Book of Poetry,* which will be released in the future. For now: Read on, and hopefully you will laugh, feel sorrow, and perhaps even recognise yourself.

Contents

Do You Recognise Yourself?

A poetry collection about people from my life
Some causing others major trouble and strife
Battle-axes who are tough and full of might
Those whose behaviour is bizarre and not right
Stock characters who you might have met
Causing your temperature to boil and sweat
Men and women who think they are desirable
But really merely entertaining and satirical
There are poems that are funny and humorous
Jenny surely cannot be real and so dubious
Other poems are both endearing and humbling;
People who certainly don't deserve mocking
Before you laugh and put this book on the shelf
Just internally ask, *Do you recognise yourself?*

16 Years Wasted on YOU and I Ain't EVER Taking You Back

It's time to tell the tale
Of how a certain male
Who worked at UK Mail
Made you old and frail

You might need a moment to exhale
The years with him you did prevail
His selfish ways on such a scale
Until he made you old and stale

Sixteen years with you, oh why?
Internally you made me cry
You've aged me to need hair dye
So Fuck off now, that's right, goodbye

It's time to tell the tale of how you made her old
From that young woman who once was bold
Controlled and cajoled you made her kinda mould
When you should have treated her like gold

Sixteen years with him, he gave you children too
So he must have had some clue
On treating you right and true
But slowly, slowly he became your one taboo

It's time to tell the tale of what he put you through
He stifled you to have no view
That man belongs now in a zoo
For making you feel so damned subdued

The bed we should have shared
A man and woman couple-paired
You lacked displays that showed you cared
That chapter now completely tarred

Throw me off a mountain
Drown me in a fountain
Stick me in gale force winds and rain
Rather than listen to you whinge and complain

To save our relationship I did strive
Your work you continued to abuse and skive
You slept your life away instead of being alive
My love for you destroyed, and that you cannot revive

A tale of how you made me old and grey
Refusing your children clothes to pay
Shouting and cursing causing you to fray
Is why our relationship ended 2015 in May

But just to clarify we did not fail
Our kids we have to hail
Make ourselves to them avail
But you? You can go and fucking sail

Sixteen years with you
I need to say adieu
To start my life anew
To stop us feeling blue

Learn now to fucking drive
My life I will retrieve and thrive
Whilst you continue your children to deprive
I'm free and single and know I can survive

Acute Senses

She has envious eyes
Fluttering them to disguise
All those evil lies
Deceptively she cries
To capitalise
And publicise
Falsified events that she wants to dramatise
Continuing her reign to terrorise
Yet she is unable to realise
She's the only person she truly does demonise

She takes deep breaths filling each lung
Then gets to work with that treacherous tongue
Her words are wily
Almighty and slimy

She uses her ears
To overhear
But those ears are enchanted
As new conversations are implanted

With her animated hands
She continues her plans
Going beyond the sense of touch
So much more, so much
Transferring her feelings of anxiety
With verve and ferocity
Affecting them mentally
Steering them towards insanity

She is a woman who belongs in hell
Because her sense of smell
Is like the Underworld's fire
Brutal, unrelenting and dire
For she can sniff out your fears
Reducing you to tears
Find out what you like
Then attack and strike
Like Hitler's Third Reich
She has a habit that's niche
It's her nose that does twitch
As though it has an itch
Like the 1970's Bewitched witch
But it's really because she is a bitch

Always Remember

She worked at the same company for over twenty years
Hard work and dedication would often end in tears
Unappreciated and abused by her job share colleague
Resulting in being driven to anger and work fatigue
Some of the managers were totally fucking useless
Suffering from being power-mad with rudeness
Then came the day that she was betrayed by Jenny
A short woman who is sad, pathetic and rather heavy
Spreading her malicious lies with lethal ferocity
That evil bitch whose heartless soul is a monstrosity
The woman subjected to slander, refused to become frail
Her strength and spirit rose, and forever will prevail
Because she has good friends and the best family
Who will always be there to support her thoroughly

An Elf

Weather's windy and the sky's not bright
Through the shopping centre they fight
In order to make their son's Christmas a delight
Queues in shops to buy presents feels like a plight
And then to Santa's Grotto fighting frostbite
It feels like this day won't end before midnight

Finally they meet the man in red whose beard is white
The little one begins to murmur cries at such a sight
Clinging on to his mummy with all his strength and might
But sitting on his momma's knee settles down his fright
A wrapped up present causes baby to feel excite
Now looking braver than a sovereign's knight

Quickly dressed up as an elf, actually looks quite right
Baby giggles, followed by parental smiles does ignite
Followed by a family pose and a camera's flashlight
Meeting Father Christmas for his first time worked out
  alright
And Christmas day to be celebrated in a fortnight
When extended family gathers round and does unite

Angry Man

He struts about
Parading like a silverback gorilla
Aggressively looking at staff
Ensuring that they are intimidated
He threatens to suspend them
To dismiss them
Making their life a misery

He stomps about
Like a child having a temper tantrum
Huffing and puffing
Almost like a bull in an arena
Ready to charge
Wounding his staff
With words and threats

He marches about
As though a soldier in war
But this one is certainly no hero
He is filled with anger and hate
Determined to inflict pain
Deluded that he is respected
Whereas the reality is, he is pitied and hated

Animal Magnetism

As he leaves it's time to reflect and write a guide
The traits that he used to help him lead and decide
He watched and observed as though eagle eyed
Like a lion, he roared in order to look after his pride
And like a shepherd over his flock he did preside
But sometimes his decisions caused people to divide
Even when new jobs he created and did provide
So he became tougher than a rhino's leathered hide

Working for this man is certainly no joyride
As though gathered meercats you work side by side
New skills you will learn and develop that are bona fide
Like an elephant his memory is amplified
Through the offices like a panther he does glide
His wisdom is like Athena's owl as it does not subside
Despite at times with him you did verbally collide
Quoting this man, his techniques are; results verified

Ann

There is a woman whose name is Ann
Of her writing I've become a real fan
She can write about anything, she can
Trying to eat black pudding in her van
Which had been fried in a butcher's pan
Antics of a surgery and its dentist man
Steel doors compared to a sexy woman
The life of a trout and how it began
A tale of a wife's murderous plan
She's seen quite a lot in her lifespan
Subjected to flattery by a repairman
Offer declined as he didn't look like Tarzan
I hope this rhyme will not get me a ban
From *The Time to Write* group clan
Or in anger for Ann, my behind to tan

Anxiety Beckons

My symptoms I will try to explain
Energy levels do dissipate and drain
Weighted down by an invisible chain
Head pounds stronger than a migraine
Concentration falters and does wane
Eyes struggle due to pressurised strain
Heart palpitations thump again and again
Along with blood rushing without constrain
As though under the influence of cocaine

Stomach swishes as though an empty domain
Contracting muscles spasm causing pain
Thoughts and memories collide in my brain
Which all seems stronger than torrential rain
Resulting in difficulties for my sanity to retain
Making me feel as though I will become insane
So I strive to find clarity and for that to remain
Deep breaths I take in order to calm and retrain
My efforts and endeavours all seem to be in vain

Not wanting to become a burden I do not complain
Symptoms increase and now feeling like a hurricane
Health wavers and my future I am unable to ascertain
Without physical ailments others think it's all mundane
They wonder if my symptoms I do pretend and feign
I continue to fight on for my health to regain and sustain
Ongoing internal battles and wars I try my best to detain
No one wants mental health stigma to strengthen and gain
One day I hope anxiety and stress levels to control and contain

A Poem to Frustrate

It was in January 1998
When that man arrived that you either love or hate
Some say his management technique was to dominate
Whereas others said that to them he did motivate
And so his reputation seems to fluctuate
But even if your morale at times seemed to deflate
The productivity certainly never did stagnate
Instead he achieved the business to become first rate

Those who wanted to progress started him to adulate
At times his mannerisms they almost seemed to imitate
After fifteen years he's now decided to abdicate
The gossiping now seems to escalate
As the staff and managers all seem to debate
Who will replace this magnate?
But they will all have to be patient and await
For now, goodbye, and hope these words have not caused
  you to feel irate

A Toothless Hag

Her one front tooth wobbles
As she eagerly gossips away
When eating something that needs a bite
She looks like a rabbit or rat
But with only one tooth
Which sways as though in the midst of a breeze

She loves her gossip and her judgemental remarks
Never acknowledging the opinions of others
Because hers are the only ones that matter
And of course she is always right
So clever and wise
In her own mind at least

Others accept her opinions
Because they don't want an angered debate
Or to suffer her wrath
Loud words so that everyone can hear
And of course ultimately they don't challenge
Because they are focused on two things

Everyone who comes in contact with this woman
Is fascinated by the size 18 outfit tops
Which manage to cling onto 20% of her body
Whilst the rest of the belly blubber and flab trembles
Just like the second thing that grabs their attention
The one and only front tooth which continues to wobble

A Young King's Birthday (version 2)

He sits and settles into his raised regal throne
It's comfortable; the King will not be overthrown
The crown is placed upon his head
But all he wants is for his mouth and stomach to be fed
Curiously gazes at his subjects to the left and to the right
And in front a candle on the birthday cake is set alight

Rowdy is the gathering today
The party is now well under way
The birthday bloke has a look of bewilderment
Open jaw and widened eyes set like cement
The presents in the hall are in abundance, quite galore
Amassed upon the party floor

The food arrives and put out on the table
Looking like a scene from some old fable
All the fuss is in this young man's honour
Yet he'll soon become his usual yawner
Because being a King on your birthday
Is kind of exhausting after kids play

Baby With the Bright Blue Eyes (extended version)

Eyes so blue and bright
My life you re-ignite
In my arms I hold you tonight
My baby son so warm and light
You look at me and giggle with delight
Making me feel so proud and … well just right
And as you grow up in height
So many things I'll teach you if that's alright

With your mum you'll learn to read and write
We'll even teach you how your food to bite
Take you to a camping site
Be near you when you fly a kite
And train you up to have real might
Advising you on women who make you feel excite
Show you how to drive, even when weather's kinda shite
But never forgetting manners and being polite

Your image will always be in my mind and sight
Unconditional Love I give you as a rite
Inner demons I will help you fight
Making sure your life you do not blight
Listening and protecting you when in a plight
As you go to sleep, eyes closed so tight
I'm still here, beside you day and night
Until you're a man and no longer our little mite

Beach Boys

They met each other almost two years ago
Devoted and inseparable; the beach boy duo
In the swimming pool they put on a show
Playing and laughing beneath the sun's glow
They pose in front of a woman they know
As she clicks on a camera taking their photo

Similar clothes the beach boys seem to wear
Even in swimwear sitting on a deck chair
Or strutting around as though debonair
The older one lifts the younger one in mid-air
And the woman who knows them both is there
As she takes another photo of this golden pair

She looks at the young men with admiration
Before joining them in close congregation
Together they pose for a new photo occasion
Looking as though in the middle of a celebration
Heart rates beating with exhalation and excitation
The man, his wife and son, on their holiday vacation

Beautiful

She knows that she is beautiful
Men hit on her throughout the day
Wanting her in their bed
She knows just what they want
She knows just what to do
To get whatever she wants
Without succumbing to their advances

She flirts and smiles
Chit-chats and giggles
Makes jokes and laughs
Showing off her good nature
And in return
She has an easy life

She knows she occupies their minds
Naughty scenes in their imagination
But the closest thing they'll get
Is her scent and laughter
Her company
And nothing more

She knows that other women are envious
They start their rumours
Giving her dirty looks
Ignoring her
All because they pale in comparison
To her personality and beauty

Boys in Blue

There are these two men who are strolling
Through the countryside
They're both dressed in blue
With a husky dog on a lead
They take in the view
Of autumn coloured leaves
Whilst making their way through marshy woodland

The tall man talks and talks
Whilst the shorter younger one listens
He occasionally makes a suckling sound
And sometimes
Just sometimes
Nods off to sleep
As his father pushes him along in his pram

Brexit

Brave words of Brexit
Spoken over and over
"We are leaving on the 29th March 2019"
"We will be leaving on October 31st, Deal or No Deal"
"Brexit means Brexit"
"We need to get on and deliver Brexit"
"No deal is better than a bad deal"
"No deal is catastrophic for this country"
"We hold all the cards"
"It is not in the interests of the European Union"
"The free trade agreement ….with the European Union….
  will be one of the easiest in human history"
"It is the will of the people"
"I represent my constituents"
"There will be no changes to the backstop"
"The backstop needs to go"
"This house needs to…"
"I will not ask for an extension"
"I will abide by the law"
"I strongly disagree with the judgment of the judiciary"
"If you have not secured a deal will you request an
  extension?"
"I am not inclined to do so"
"It needs to go to a people's vote"
"The people have spoken"
"I represent the people"
"This is a dead parliament"
"This is a paralysed parliament"
"The Prime Minister needs to resign"

"The opposition leader needs to resign"
"I have removed the Tory Whip"
"We are united as one"
"This is a domestic issue for the United Kingdom"
"I will be pushing for a second referendum on Scottish
    Independence"
"It is unconstitutional to prorogue parliament"
"We need to prorogue parliament because we need a
    Queen's speech"
"Will the Prime Minister apologise to Her Majesty for
    misleading her?"
"There is only one chlorinated chicken in this house"
It is the rollercoaster ride of political satire
That has become known across the world as Brexit

Broken Marriage

She stays with him
In the same home
But different bedrooms
Not due to loyalty
Love or even the children
It is the shame
The culture that she comes from
That she remains
Unhappy and unfulfilled
Tormented, distressed and depressed

He stays with her
For similar reasons
He would rather kill her
Than live in a separate house
Divorce is a dirty word
He drinks to excess
Drowning his thoughts
Becoming more and more broken
Beating her with his fists
Ensuring that she remains subservient

Her life
Including happiness
Starts from the moment she steps outside the front door
It doesn't matter whether there is sunshine or rain
She'll flirt with men
Be obvious and blatant
Which leads to affairs galore
Fulfilling her ardent desires
Until she returns at night
To her broken marriage

Bye-Bye

The time is almost nigh
For that final handshake and goodbye
To the man who watched you with his eagle eye
In order to ensure your work to his standards did comply

Do you need another clue in order to identify?
Just who these words do exemplify
One look from him and your work rate would intensify
Yes, I'm on about that senior manager guy

So let's quickly digest and clarify
The characteristics of this man that you cannot deny
Your areas of improvement he would qualify and quantify
But when needed your strengths he would gratify and
  fortify

When he leaves will your eyes cry or be dry?
I hope you do not just stand by
Instead a farewell that will him glorify
The man who regularly his beard does dye

Cars

Does what car you own
Explain who you are?
A mini showing that you are
A classy person
Or just small statured
And without much money?

Does a sports car show
That you are athletic and fit
Or just a lifestyle that you aspire to?

What if you drive a Mercedes
A Jaguar or a Lamborghini?
That shows that you have money
Doesn't it?
Or perhaps it is your parents
Who are loaded?
Maybe owning such a car
Has put you in debt
Or perhaps you are a car jacker
And you're taking such a car
For a joyride and a spin

Chunky

There is a guy I know who I call Chunky
He's got fatted cheeks
Crawls on all fours
Got a pot-belly like a piglet
Makes snorting noises
Just one look at him and he makes me smile
Which then makes him giggle and laugh
My baby son
My little Chunky

Colour of Her Hair

She walks into work with her new hairstyle
Vibrant colours which she mixed herself
As psychedelic as the drugs that she takes
Marching towards her intended destination
Through the forest of intimidating stares
Whilst listening to the acid-toned whispers

"Grotbags is here"
"Is that a mop on her head?"
"She looks like Orville"
"I'm thinking of having green giant peas today."
"Attention seeker"
"Look what colour the bitch has dyed her hair"

Her smile widens
High on weed
She struts her booty
And pouts her lips
Making sure that everyone knows
I'm here to stay and fuck you all

Cuddle

Parents, uncles, aunts and strangers all seem to want a cuddle
But sometimes I just want to go to my cot to sleep and snuggle
When I was younger I only wanted to suckle
Now I see them arrive and I think, *'Here's trouble'*
I try to scramble away by shuffle or scuttle
But they grab and hold me with all of their muscle
So my efforts I mightily increase and double
And it looks as though we're engaged in a bit of a tussle

There's no use in trying to juggle or struggle
Because they hold me so tight, it's as though we're a couple
They start to pull faces as though blowing a bubble
Waiting and watching for me to show them a chuckle
And if it's an uncle or a granddad I can feel their stubble
One day you wait, I'll be able to get away by waddle
Then I'll learn speech to be able to answer you all by rebuttal
It will be with good humour as I don't want your feelings to
   ruffle

You start to walk away and wanting you back I start to be subtle
My lower lip trembles and in my nappies I begin to feel a puddle
Please! Wait! Come back and make funny sounds like a ruckle
Or maybe shake my favourite rattle and give me a huddle
I suppose you must think that I am full of befuddle
But I'm young and so excuse me for being a little bit fickle
Lifting me up, I smile as I have learned how to hustle
And bury my face against you whilst giving you a great big
   cuddle

Diva

To those that she wants something from
And those that she merely wants
She is endearing, complimentary and flirty
Alluring, provocative and sultry in her sexiness
These are just some of the tools that she uses
To get exactly what she wants and who she wants

Then there is her reaction to others
The ones that she cannot stand or even tolerate
She doesn't hide her dislike of them
Argumentative, temper tantrums, and rudeness
Silent, sullen, and facial expressions of disgust
Because they can't give her the things she wants

She believes that she is special and deserves attention
That she should be showered with expensive gifts
Living a luxurious life without having to work
If she is not given what she wants and when she wants it
She transforms from sweet and soft to sour and sadistic
All because she's a demonstratively demanding diva

Duped

There is a type of person
Who exhibits charm and charisma
Appears to be so hard working
Attentive to detail
Meeting deadlines
Yet all the time
They are continually deceiving
Stealing ideas and work of others
Taking credit when they have done nothing
Being corrupt to the extreme

Lies spurn out of their mouths like air
Yet appear realistic and truthful
Surrounding themselves
By those who can further their careers
Using their own limited powers
To pursue the ones they want to bed
And truly demean and punish those they dislike
Whilst all the time
Continue to appear professional
Even though they are the antithesis of professionalism

The standards they display are impressive
Despite their own standards
Being morally and ethically reprehensible
The men and women
Who are able to dupe people
Due to their pathological sociopathic personality
Continue to progress
Spurred on by their hunger
For power and authority
Who is brave enough to expose the reality?

Entrapment

His addiction was beautiful women
Who he chased unrelentingly
Despite being married
And having a regular mistress
He continued with his obsession
Woman after woman
Would succumb
To his charms and charisma
Heightened and extreme arousal and seduction
Wanton and wild antics would ensue
Expert in his craft
Ensuring sexual satisfaction

Experience did not alert him
To what would happen next
A young temptress
Alluring and provocative
Texts he would send her
Like the ones he sent to others
She led him like a dog on a lead
Collecting evidence which she used
Getting revenge for her best friend
Who he had slept with and discarded
Too arrogant to see what was happening
That he was the one being entrapped

Evil Man

Arrogant, smarmy, cynical, cruel and evil
He instils fear in people by shouting at them
Asserting his leadership with attack precision
Comparable to the ferocity of a wild beast
Whereas a lion savagely kills another animal
And then feasts upon its meat
This man has a unique form of cannibalism
For he murders and devours the human psyche and resolve
Merely for entertainment purposes
Humiliation and threats are just two of the tools he uses
To destroy and annihilate their spirit
Determined to make them subservient and inferior
Ensuring that his superiority complex is justified

The bullying methodology he uses
Is instinctive and inventive
Due to the years of experience he's had to perfect them
Compassion and behaving with dignity and respect
Is non-existent in his world
There are no boundaries of criticism or tactics that he will
  use
Even when the person has died
As a direct consequence of his actions
He shows and feels no remorse
Because he believes that he is truly omnipotent
That others should blindly follow his instructions
Showering him with compliments, adulation and
  admiration
Whilst cowering in temperament and operating like a
machine

He thinks that he is a ladies man
That women find him attractive and sexy
Drawn to his power, charm and wit
Even though the reality is, they are repulsed
By the ugliness of his personality and the absence of a
  human soul
But he continues to make overt sexual remarks and gestures
Sordid, slobbering and rapey in his inept enthusiasm
Not to mention just staring at their breasts
Even when in high profile meetings
He walks as though he is a King
Walking amongst the poorest of his subjects
Judging them without knowing them
Disgusted by their low status

He doesn't mind being hated
So long as they are also fearful of him
With a click of his fingers
He'll find an excuse to dismiss someone
Not bothered of the life-changing circumstances that will
  cause them
Thrown into insecurity and unable to pay their essential
  bills
Spiralling into depression and desolation
All because he has no conscious
That evil man who is a sociopath
Oblivious to any code of moral or ethical standards
Believing that laws, rules and regulations do not apply to
  him
Ultimately, as far as he is concerned
His decisions are the law

Evil Woman

The look she gives
That's full of glare and stare
As though in a trance
Where she is focused on her evil spell
To fill your life with torment and pain
Her fires of hell unleashed

Yet with those who she thinks can further her career
She laughs and tolerates their humour
A different kind of magic that she uses
To gain their trust and loyalty
Totally unaware of her ambitions and intentions
To take their power, strength and even their career

Being firm and fair dissipates
Along with codes of ethics and morality
Replaced by her own brand of rules and regulations
The triple rule of R:
Be ruthless, rude and unrelenting
Break their spirit and their morale

She enjoys watching her underlings suffer
Silent, meek and broken
Not to mention those whose careers she has destroyed
Merely to entertain her evil essence
But nothing can camouflage that stare and glare
A face that is sour-soaked and bitter-baked

Eyes (extended version)

I look into those widened eyes
The ones that seduce young guys
Like a spell those men you hypnotise
They're yours to sexually demoralise
And marriages you do destabilise

Ten years from now, I look into your eyes
Obviously older now, but still unwise
You seduce men as your ultimate prize
But one sure thing you do not realise
Is that your life, others begin to satirise

Others are watching you through their eyes
Fulfilling dreams that they can only fantasise
Your conquest numbers continue to rise
They return to their wives which you criticise
Then move onto other victims to immobilise

Looking in the mirror at your own eyes
Can you remember and memorise
All those lives that you did scandalise
Or do you still completely rationalise
And feel your life others should epitomise

Twenty years from now those beautiful eyes
Will be worn out from all those tearful cries
You'll have run out of the seduction lies
And even with mascara you cannot disguise
That over your life you do now agonise

Fire

A quiet guy
Intelligent and wise
With humour the size of mountains
Always seeing the best in people
Timid and accepting of others
Kindness in abundance
Never annoyed
Instead a constant smile
A genuine laugh
Happy-go-lucky in life

It was a woman
Who brought out the fire
He felt it in his belly
Or rather in his abs
For he was a man of skin
Sliding over bones
His temperament altered
At first a mild curry level
Eventually hot spices and peppers
Being added

The intelligence and wisdom
Was clearly still there
Very much enshrined into his personality
But those flames were spreading
A wild fire beneath
Adding tolerance and a sharp bite
To his once innocent tongue
A tongue that had tasted the fire of her
Oriental delights
Sometimes sizzling and other times scorching

Fires of the Liar

She wants to climb the ranks higher and higher
Totally obsessed it has become her sole desire
Internally within her mind she does conspire
Masquerading her incompetence she does require
And discrediting her rivals she wants to transpire

Without remorse she lights up an invisible fire
Telling tales and lies which if believed are dire
Her victims feel the inferno heat and do perspire
Destroying the reputation of her competitor highflier
It has become her craft to be a pathological liar

Hidden fires burn and burn like a funeral pyre
Lie upon lie, fire upon fire, she never does tire
In her behaviour enemies she does acquire
Because innocent people are caught in the crossfire
The energy she uses you could almost admire

Her antics are a frequent source for humorous satire
If caught out she'll feign distress becoming a crier
She never learns and resorts to what she has done prior
Malicious techniques she adapts in order not to expire
Relighting volcano lies which erupt due to being a liar

Funeral Song

I want to choose my funeral song
Something appropriate and memorable
It's so easy to choose songs for other people
Elizabeth Taylor and Zsa Zsa Gabor both should have had
Going to the Chapel and We're Gonna Get Married
Pity that song didn't exist when Henry VIII was buried
Although *Eight is The Magic Number* also seems ideal
Of course Nelson Mandela certainly deserves *Freedom*
Muhammad Ali should have had either
Eye of the Tiger or *We are the Champions*

Donald Trump will obviously want *I Did it My Way*
And maybe he could pre-record *Push the Button* just for
Kim Jong-un
Nigel Farage and Boris Johnson should have *Rule
 Britannia*
David Attenborough ought to have *The Lion Sleeps Tonight*
In fact he should also have the hymn, *All Creatures Great
 and Small*
If they ever rebury Elizabeth I she could have *Like a Virgin*
Unlike Hugh Hefner who should've had *House of the
Rising Sun*
A totally new meaning of *Maggie May* for Margaret
 Thatcher
I'm sure all records would have been broken
If the Iron Lady and Arthur Scargill did a duet
Those Were the Days and *Working in a Coal Mine* might
 have been their songs

Jackie Kennedy Onassis would have probably chosen
Devil in Disguise for Marilyn Monroe
Perhaps Hilary Clinton should have *Stand By Your Man*
Especially after her spat with Tammy Wynette
But back to MY funeral song
Always Look on the Bright Side of Life is not loud enough
I was leaning towards *Staying Alive*
But in the end I decided to take into consideration where
  I'll end up
Not the original meaning of the song, but hey ho
  Sound of the Underground

Gamesmaster

He's stuck in a bygone era
Where board games are mainstream
Forget the computer games
This man is the King of board games

He has an excellent humour
A fantastic family man
Work ethic
With a positive outlook on life

Yet when he has visitors
After the ample and delicious food
Out comes the board games
Box after box after box

It's the same when he visits others
Lots of board games
From the boot of his car
The back seat and laps of his family

Then the true nature comes out
His competitive streak
The lively antics and the challenging begins
Determined to win

Gentle

In an age
Where arguments and raised voices
Are considered part of normal life
You do not come across many
Who are calm and gentle

Others consider that there is something wrong
A man who is a man of few words
Maybe he is autistic or has Asperger's
Perhaps just not street savvy
Or even an idiot

Yet that man is the one who is intelligent
Those few words spoken
Often wise and advisory
Without being patronising or judgmental
Pure kindness of a gentleman

Gobby Cow

She talks fast
Not allowing anyone else to talk
Loud and shrieking voice
That is opinionated and rude
Almost as though
Covering up her insecurities
Her temper is unrestrained
Quite in contrast to her small stature
You can hear her
Before you actually see her
Stomping along
Putting the world to rights
The never-ending shrill
Of the migraine-giving
Gobby cow

Great Britain

From the depths of despair, anger and desolation
Day by day, brick by brick; we lay down the foundation
In order to rise again, and become a great nation
Through times that are rough and tough
We will strive to proceed and succeed
New opportunities we will seek
We will not remain meek or weak
Our strengths we will use
Weaknesses we will reduce
And threats we will defuse

As the links with the EU Union we unweave
History shows us what we can achieve
World wars we have fought and won
The Empire and Commonwealth we have run
Pioneers in ensuring people have their rights
Are just a few of our historical highlights
A new period of negotiation and trade we now face
That future we will boldly and proudly embrace
For we are Great Britain, and that you cannot erase or
  efface
We will gain our premier place through decorum and grace

Courage will ensure we build a new golden age
With the entire globe we are now able to engage
Continue being an essential part of the world stage
Remain or Leave voters and campaigners will unite
With increased passion and vigour we'll show might
Burning fires within our hearts and minds will ignite
As we will reach and create new power and wealth
Invest in our people to promote stability and good health
Despite the prediction of doom and gloom through fear
We will become triumphant because we persevere

Great to Grate

It's time to reflect upon what has happened and the truth to
finally orate
For weeks campaigners argued 'remain' or 'leave' and
gave it to us straight
All those many days where men and women engaged in
heated debate
In order to decide the future of Great Britain in the
European Union state
Boris, Farage, and Cameron all say they want to make
Britain Great

To the polls the people go, to cast their vote and a
referendum decision to create
Through the night voters listen to their television screens
making bedtime very late
Graphs of the voting, like in a General Election, they
continue to show in order to illustrate
Then the outcome is announced and those in favour of EU
'Leave' now start to celebrate
Unaware of what is about to transpire to Great Britain, Great
Britain, Great...

The pound, hour by hour, begins its decline and its strength
does depreciate
The value of stocks and shares not only fluctuate but
actually just decimate
Experts discuss on the news about what will occur to the
bank's interest rate
An isolated island. All alone. Abandoned. Desolate.
Once known as Britain. A nation that was great.

But weep for all those who left loved ones and to Britain
did migrate
Wanting a better life, but now become victims of
campaigns of hate
Ignorant people, hiding behind cowardly written notes,
demanding others to repatriate
Did you think there would be no consequence for the
voting bomb that you did detonate?
A once tolerant nation. No longer considered to be great.

The decline continues with speed and does accelerate
The EU demanding Article 50 and to immediately
disassociate
So that they become twenty-seven countries instead of
twenty-eight
Foreign companies their headquarters to other countries
they will relocate
In one fell swoop Britain is shredded. Great Britain. Grate
Britain. Grate....

Guided

There are clichés
About how powerful love is
How love is blind
In my case the words to describe our relationship
Is *guided*

I was guided like a dog by its owner
The lead was strong and sturdy as steel
And the hand that held the lead was rigid
Guiding me to change my life
To be moulded and manufactured

Our love was real and authentic
I used to be an agnostic
But changed my beliefs to Islam
Each decision precipitated by her words
Which were soothing and full of warmth

Yet eventually I came to realise
That whilst I was willing to make sacrifices
Make changes and wield to her requests
She was not able to make the slightest alteration
Everything had to be on her terms

There were tears if I did not do precisely as asked
But she was just as much a victim of the curse of being
  guided
For she had been guided all of her life
And love is genuinely blind after all
Because she was unable to see those tough invisible leashes

HCB

She's practiced her infamous femme fatale strut walk
Unfortunately she can't control her shriek vocal talk
She's had her cheeks and buttocks lifted by surgery
And other imperfections altered by medical sorcery

Such as lips enhanced by collagen which she does pout
Even though those lips look as though lifted from trout
Proud she's had her breasts at least five times enlarged
To match the rest of her fake body, now camouflaged

Augmented hips
Lifted eye lids
Through all the nip and tuck tricks
Men stare as though transfixed

But the one real thing she needed to fix
She'll never be able to change or eclipse
She always has to have the last word
Causing arguments that are absurd

Spends hours at the hairdresser
This wild woman of leisure
And chases after married men
Occasionally capturing them

This woman that does bewitch
Behaving like a Hard Core Bitch
Or do you disagree?
That she is the ultimate HCB

How Many Words Can You Rhyme With Your name, Alexander?

It's time to tell the story of a guy called Alexander
Who progressed high up on the management ladder
Walking high and proud with the ultimate swagger
Whilst those who are jealous begin words of slander
Spreading false news and rumours is their propaganda
Which grow and grow like tumours which are cancer
But he doesn't react to show them what is anger
With a bellowing voice that is like thunder
Because he's calm and cool is the answer

His success as a senior manager
Was because of being a grafter
So he decided to start a new chapter
He considered becoming a rude rapper
Perhaps appearing on the show, X-Factor
Or Strictly Come Dancing as a dancer
A church sermon preaching Pastor
Ploughing the fields on a tractor
An Olympian athlete running faster and faster

This guy who goes by the name of Alexander
Enjoys talking selfies and putting them on Twitter
Different images he portrays as a comedic master
Dressed in a suit trying to look naturally dapper
Maybe as though pretending to be an actor
With pouting lips he belongs in the movie Zoolander

Or perhaps a remake starring in Ben Hur
Of course he would have to be the title character
Occasionally drunk, passed out and appearing a disaster

Then there's those photos which could be 'before and after'
Displaying his rock hard abs creates a bit of banter
Because his image and torso is now that of a body-builder
And if you haven't guessed, he is what is called a poser
Hoping this rubbish rhyme has caused that guy Alexander
To smile and chuckle, along with howling laughter

How Many Words Can You Rhyme With Your Name, Chad?

Time for silliness as we rhyme words with Chad
That guy who's always been a bit of a lad
Smiling as though always glad
Never glum-faced as though sad
Behaved in the past as though a cad
Larking about with mates as though mad
And women there's been a few that he's had
He's got maths qualifications that show he can add
On his postal walk he's shown he's as brave as Sir Galahad
In the words of Michael Jackson, *He's bad, he's bad*
He's really, really bad

So what more can we say about this man whose name is
  Chad?
He's no longer alone like a tramp or nomad
Because he's married his work colleague comrade
Their relationship growing stronger as it is now ironclad
Unless he upsets her and then watch the missile launch pad
He goes to the gym trying to become as fit and strong as an
  Olympiad
And that's when he takes selfies of being slightly unclad
Almost as though dreaming of being a model in an ad
To Lewis he has become a fantastic stepdad
Together Chad, Silvana and Lewis have become a triad
Include Ziggy and Lola for the family to increase its
  members to a myriad

p.s. It's a good job this poem isn't rhyming with your
woman's name Silvana
Because apart from where they buried Fidel Castro in
Havana
The only other rhyming word I can think of would end up
being rude because the word is banana

Hurricane

The rain outside rages into a storm and pours
Whilst the hurricane wind howls and roars
New streams created rush through the streets
Gusts and gale forces increase in their beats

The pre-school playgroup doors swing wide open
Hurricane enters causing children to be frozen
He wobbles and giggles as he makes his way
Jumping on a boy twice his age and size to play

His mother picks up her toddler-hurricane boy
Who tips his head and puts on his smile with joy
A face that screams, "I'm cool. I'm a geezer"
Melting her heart; Already a future deceiver

Ibiza

It's time to tell the tale
Of a certain beautiful female
She'll soon be a bride, but at the moment a hen
And who is she? It's the one and only Helen

Chit-chat group texts over their mobile phone
In order to decide the hen-do location zone
Majorca! Agia Napa! *Wolverhampton's Yates?*
Off to Ibiza goes this group of female mates

Then lots of discussions about what to wear
Worries about stomach fat causes them despair
But the gorgeous outfits are finally chosen
Breathe in dears, to hide any flab that's swollen

Friends and family gather at the airport
Too late now for the holiday to abort
Twenty-two women let loose without their men
To celebrate in bars, clubs, and the Ibiza ocean

Apart from giggling, what do you think they got up to?
Well get ready for the list of things, all of which are true
Meeting the brother of a former famous football star
At the Ibiza club he owns called *Linekar's Bar*

It was at Club Pacha where we were drinking and laughing
And who could forget Aunty Cougar's excelling at pole
  dancing
A lounge given to us by someone wanting an invite to the
  wedding

Free drinks by a Pit-Bull lookalike; famous for his singing

As for the outfits who could forget the Greek-themed
  party?
Dressed in togas and behaving badly, not like the doll
  called Barbie
Given nicknames to reflect our nature
Met a man who although a stranger:

Ended up agreeing to strip down nude
Took off his clothes with attitude
Whilst danced as though being screwed
Our eyes fixated on what we viewed
A frolicking naked man that is no prude
This might sound as though it's crude
Or even mighty lewd
But truly he had our eyes glued
Putting us in a sexy dancing mood
Can you imagine what he did that was rude?
Something flopping I do conclude
A woman's hand then did protrude
Determined to touch and intrude
His rock hard bum she then pursued
He was unable her hand to elude
But he didn't feel devalued
Continued dancing in solitude
With increased strength and fortitude
Almost as though in gratitude
Everyone's dance was now renewed
With intensified magnitude

But that is just part of the story
Chained to a man showing all his glory
At least he was just made of plastic
Wearing a necklace made of tampons was fantastic
Given to you by an aunty named *The Devil*
You wore it with pride as though a medal

Stayed out till five in the morning
Causing us all to be yawning
Back to reality we go
Along with photos and video
Wishing you all the best for the future
Filled with health, happiness and humour

I Do Not Wish to Interfere, But I Do Want to Be a Friend

I do not wish to hurt you
But your life you need to review
Your marriage has no value
When your husband kicks you with his shoe

I wish your life from a distance you could view
To see impartially what he has put you through
You are treating your children as your relationship glue
Yet he'll humiliate you again, it's the cycle of déjà vu

You should never be hit, or have to hide the black and blue
It's easy for me to say, I know that's true
It takes strength and courage to say to him adieu
In order for your life to start anew

What he does to you should be taboo
Don't want you to be another statistic corpse statue
Wiping my tears at your funeral with a tissue
Instead, a new life I hope you do pursue

Ignoring Laws

I work for a company that I used to love and adore
They no longer abide by their own policies or the law
So who do I go to for advice via letter, e-mail or a phone
  call?
The unions want your money but that's just about all
Management caused your mind to decay and withdraw
Grievances take months and years and that's a major flaw
So you type away at the keyboard with your own paws
Sending the details to the ones you respected and were in
  awe
But they do not respond and your faith drops to the floor
Your options now are limited and your health you want to
  restore
You look at your years at work and the injustices are quite
  galore
Invisible tears and bleeding from a shattered heart does pour
For you are discarded, and your rights they do ignore
Perhaps I should ask the Prime Minister to actually explore
Why the organisations whose profits increase and soar
Behave in an unprofessional manner which society should
  abhor

In Love

From a very young age
He fell in love
Captivated by her beauty
Devoting time and effort to capture her
Their love affair becoming overwhelming
Fingers tenderly caressing her curvaceous body

It was a love that was reciprocal
As she blossomed
Gaining more and more pounds
They worked well together
A home they built
With nice furniture

He never forgot
The first time he was attracted to her
Just five shillings in his hand
At the age of four
Led to his one and only true love
Money, money, money

Inspirational

He talks as though truly inspirational
Believing that his life is aspirational
With confidence he seduces women to his bed
Influencing men with tales that should remain unsaid
He has become a legend within his own mind
To reality he has become oblivious and blind

He will not be remembered in history
Like Churchill's speech leading to victory
A cigar-gravelled voice over the airwaves
Inspiring to free those captured like slaves
Or Martin Luther King who had a dream
His words bringing an end to a cruel regime

She behaves as though she is a woman who knows it all
Believing that others should pander to her beck and call
Treating everyone else as though stupid and inferior
Obsessed with her own beauty which is merely her exterior
She too has become a legend within her own mind
Narcissistic, uncaring, selfish, wicked and unkind

Her soul, like Hitler and Ghengis Khan, is rotten
When she dies she will quickly be forgotten
That lip-pouting and selfie-taking diva
Whereas Florence Nightingale and Mother Teresa
Will be remembered and honoured for their devotion
Inspiring change through their acts filled with emotion

Vera Lynn motivating soldiers through her tones
Giving encouragement to millions of unknowns
Creative and philosophical poetry from Maya Angelou
Providing wisdom in aspects of life including what's taboo
Volunteers helping others with no expectation of wages to
    earn;
Time, patience, and understanding with nothing asked for
    in return

Whether wicked or benign
We alone our lives define
We are the narrator
Of our own character
Through words and actions
And even social interactions

How we react to what occurs around us
Will be reflected in what others discuss
Take a look at how yourself you treat and view
Are your actions based on self-gain and value?
Reflect on how others might be affected
And begin a selfless life that is corrected

Inter-Faith Love

I used to be an atheist
No proof of the existence of God
Philosophy readings offered the truth
We exist, we think, we make our own choices
Others influence and affect our lives
But ultimately;
Drivers of our own destiny

I fell in love with an Orthodox starlet
We were teenagers
Seventeen I think
We did what young lovers did
But then her family found out
It was made clear what options we had

To be together I had to decide
Readings and teachings from their local priest
I got baptised and a Christian I became
An engagement party followed
Two years later we drifted apart
My sacrifices all in vain

I fell in love with a young Muslim woman
Secretly we met and our love did blossom
My heart and soul given life and zest
We laughed and chit-chatted
But always made clear that for a future
There were changes that I would have to make

Books and webpages I was given to read
Mentors selected for me to develop
Answers galore on any questions I had
Giving clarity on all things Islam and faith
Steered towards the truth of existence
Rules, regulations and reformation

Once I had my own code of values
Now I follow the regimented truth
All for love and to gain approval
In secret we continued to meet and plan
Including when to tell her family our intentions

Voices of previously held views diminish
They waft away like a candle unlit
Buried deep into a tomb of silence
Secrets for protection are not lies
Honesty is modified, again to protect
Just like denials and watered-down reality

Manoeuvred into her family's trust
As we say our prayers together
Guided into Islam
Whilst all the time each and every move
Orchestrated by love
Dancing to her melodious tune

In the Dark

It's soul destroying
The not knowing
Mind scanning a multitude of possibilities
An infinity of scenarios
Stopping him from being able to sleep
Unable to eat or drink
Not caring about his own hygiene

He wants the best outcome
But will settle just to see her again
Which will stop the current pain
An e-mail, a text or even just a passed on message
To know that she is alright
Instead he's still in the dark

Her dad knows something
Her brothers too
But they are avoiding him
They want the best for her
To keep them apart
Which is breaking his heart

He wants to know what's happening
That she is healthy and happy
Instead he continues to be in the dark
Now consuming him
Barely living
In the dark

It Grunts

It walks
Able to make facial expressions
Usually the negative types
A look of disgust
Or embarrassment

No matter how many times I try to get it to talk
It merely stares
Unable to grasp my communication
Instead it staggers out of the room
Dragging its feet along
Incapable of lifting those legs

Occasionally
Just occasionally
I do get a verbal response
Like that of a gorilla or other ape
It pulls a face
As though about to huff and puff
Then the sound is released
As my teenage son
Grunts

Jane

There is a woman whose name is Jane
Her face shows that she's under strain
She looks as though she's in constant pain
All because of a fact she cannot feign
I suppose you want to know why her strength does wane
It's because she's turning 60, **shhhuuu**, AGAIN

Cheer up woman, this is not a life strain
You're not old relying on a wooden cane
Or barking mad and totally insane
You've got your smarts within that brain
It is time to live life without restrain
So much more that you can still attain

Go on holiday on the Orient Express train
Become a harem bride to someone rich in Bahrain
Do something naughty and adventurous in Spain
In Australia's Brisbane do something mundane
And other places to visit which rhyme with your name
Such as the Ukraine or New England's Maine

Do something out of the ordinary and stop being so plain
Like sky diving and parachute jumping out of a plane
Shock everyone by dancing and singing nude in the rain
Smoke weed or snort a couple of lines of cocaine
Give it a try and stop being so prim, proper and vain
May you sustain and maintain your bad behaviour reign

If you are still reading this shit I question whether you are
  still sane
Celebrate your 60th with a bottle of champagne
And even though a new wonderful life you could pave
There is something I really do need to explain
It's something secret. Mysterious. Arcane.
You're 10 minutes older now, dear Jane

Janet

Today is the birthday of a woman called Janet
Who might as well be from another planet
Eating weird healthy food like a pomegranate
She's modern using things like an iPad gadget
Posting pictures of her garden on the internet
But her speciality is being a fantastic poet
Treating the *Time to Write* group to her talent
Such as the Birmingham Floozie who got all wet
Tantalisingly being drawn to chocolate like a magnet
Describing the elderly as having facial skin like granite
Then feeding her writer friends to a desert banquet
Who then all despair wanting to go on a diet
As they struggle to get back into their jacket
Hoping this bad rhyme is not considered a hatchet
Driving you straight to the liqueur, *Golden Doublet*
Or punching me in the face with a large packet

Jekyll and Hyde Woman

There is the real life case
Of the Jekyll and Hyde woman
She is no doctor
But she is a monster
To those who can progress her career
She smiles, jokes with, and compliments
To her underlings she becomes a monster
Grotesque attitude, demeaning them with words
Making them feel like a rag doll being thrown about
Threatening, bullying and ridiculing
A malformed personality
Far worse than a sociopath or psychopath
Wicked and evil to the extreme
Lacking empathy, compassion and understanding
Able to teach the devil nouveau techniques
Petite Jekyll woman dressed in Satan's colours
A red blouse showing her cleavage
Tight black mini skirt and boots with which she stomps
Malignant Hyde creature devoid of human features
Fooling the elite into believing how wonderful she is
Standing tall on the lifeless bodies of her victims

Jenny

There is woman whose name is Jenny
She's sad, she's ugly and rather heavy
I know it sounds like I am being mean
But she really is a fucking drama queen

Expertly she does pretend
To be a good and true friend
Then backstabs is the trend
I wish to Hell she'd ascend

She thinks she is really smart
This woman who has no heart
Trying to make lives fall apart
That bitchy delusional fucktard

Always bloody bitching and moaning
I'm not exaggerating or even joking
Perhaps if she ate a little less food
That would put her in a better mood

Lambrini Girl

You drink cheap wine
The type that leaves the taste
Of anti-freeze in your mouth
Wearing shoes which makes you
Waver as you walk
Your perfume
Is a knock-off
Just like your personality

Drinking from a flute glass
Does not make you High Class
Nor does having manicures
Fake suntan shows you're fake
You wear cheap clothes
Because you are cheap
You dream of driving a Lamborghini
Just stick to drinking your Lambrini

Little Boy, Big Man

He is small statured
Well groomed
Posh accent
Used to being spoiled
All of his life

He struts
With his smarmy attitude
Arrogance surrounds him
In abundance
Dictator in every sense

Enjoys manipulating
Covering up his lies
Surrounded by *yes men*
And in his mind
He is a tall King

Yet the smallest adult-sized suits
Are at least two sizes too big
This adult man now looking
Like a little boy wearing
His daddy's clothes

Little Man Syndrome

The Little Man Syndrome
Manifests itself in a variety of ways
Child-like temper tantrums
Hungry for success, power and money
To be considered the very best
Put others down
With acidic words
In order to feel important and in control
Standing on a balcony
Looking down on others
Bringing a conceited secret smile to their face
Stomping their way through life
As though some elegant and magnificent stallion
When really just looking pitiful and small

Looks Can Be Deceiving

She looks like she belongs in the film
One Hundred Million Years B.C.
Not for being a stunner
Like Raquel Welsh
But for having a dishevelled Neanderthal look
With her long wild hair
Which looks like it's part-permed
Part-electrified
Thick, frizzy and frenzied

Yet the cliché
That looks can be deceiving
Is so true
She might not look intelligent
Silent as a mute
Looking as though brooding
And she certainly doesn't look after her appearance
A natural look
For a female version
Of Stig of the Dump

But if you talk to her
You'll find out that she's not mute
She's got intelligence
More than most
She has her own opinions
She doesn't boast about her life
The fact that she's well-travelled
Having taught English to hundreds of people
All over the world

She's seen the horrors of war
Held the hands of those who are dying
Warm hands which start to shiver
Before the rigid ice settles in
Those same hands which have dug shallow graves
Held newly discovered artefacts
From archaeological sites in Africa, Australia,
Crete, Egypt, England, and so many other countries
All rich memories that occupy her thoughts

She has a small range of books at home
On the life of Florence Nightingale
The poems of Wilfred Owen
Excavations of Heinrich Schliemann
War novels including *All Quiet On the Western Front*
And even the mammoth *War and Peace*
Turning the pages of these books
Which she's read over and over again
In the same flat she's lived in all of her life

Macho Men

They strut around work
As though omnipotent Gods
The women are there for them to seduce
To pander to their egos
And satisfy their sexual desires
They enjoy bragging
About their conquests and their manhood
Believing that their bodies are perfect
Proud to show photos of themselves in the nude
Shameless in all that they do

They gather together like a pack of wolves
Attending nightclubs and private parties
Satisfying one of their addictions
By surrounding and hungrily devouring their victims
The other two addictions being power and drugs
Cocaine and weed flowing through their bodies
Blood pumping and throbbing confidence and relaxation
Their powerful positions they abuse
Offering jobs, promotions and overtime
To get their conquests to succumb

They get promoted themselves
Through fraudulent activities
And by protecting each other
If caught out, they will lie and cheat
Creative in their explanations
Exceptionally convincing
Blaming others and making them into scapegoats

Or transforming the accuser
Into a calculating slanderous evil person
Destroying their life in the process

If someone is a threat
Genuinely hardworking and intelligent
Deserving of a promotion
Or doesn't fit into their macho fraternity
Then that pack of wolves will attack
With unrelenting ferocity
Breaking the spirit of perceived enemies
And ruining their careers
They advance only their own family and friends
In order to protect the core macho men clique

Charm and charisma is part of what they use
They are oblivious to the reality
Of how they are truly perceived
Day after day, and year after year
They continue with their macho image
Even when encountering setbacks
The macho male mentality continues to flourish
Echoing the perished phoenix
Which dramatically rises from the flames
Refreshed and ravenous for action

Mail to Male

There is a young guy who worked at UK Mail
Going to the gym trying to look like a Chippendale
Gaining abs and muscles; the opposite of looking frail
Taking selfies which just about hides his Holy Grail
On social media there are photos of him drinking ale
Jack Daniels, brandy, wines, and even a cocktail
But there is so much more to reveal in his tale
Rising up the management ladder to a heightened scale
Advising his managers on how to improve by e-mail
Leading to the company no longer having a regular record
 of fail
But his efforts were all in vain and to no avail

This could have resulted in the six foot tall man beginning
to wail
Going out drinking, fighting and end up being a victim of
 an assail
He could've become depressed, eating until looking like a
beached whale
However, he was told to "man-up" by his beloved female
Then offers started to flood in as though he was on sale
Regaining his mojo like a dog waggling his tail
Or a guy smoking with deep breaths as he inhales and
 exhales
So this man you ought to hail
Now if you've had enough humour and regale
Not to mention too much detail
Then it's time for this story to curtail
About that entertaining youthful male

Mandy

There's a heavenly woman called Mandy
Whose persona is sweeter than candy
Causing all men to become really randy
As they flex their muscles to show they are manly
Admirers includes the half-Lithuanian who's lanky
At work she is multi-skilled which is handy

Her parents are from the country of Ghandi
She enjoys drinking JD and brandy
Or even a bit of Chianti
She is always so perky and dandy
To her nephews and nieces a modern cool aunty
Unlike the ones that she works with, who're always so
   fussy and cranky

Man of Bronze

The man of steel
Built like rock
Flies through the air
Fights supervillains
Men want to be him
Powerful and strong
Whilst the women want to be with him

Iron Man is invincible
Wearing his iron suit
He also flies and fights supervillains
Worth billions
Attends parties galore
And as for the women
There may be a few he hasn't been with

There is a man of bronze
He attends the gym fanatically
Ensuring his body is strong
Just like the man of steel
But he is the man of bronze
As he steps out of the tanning salon
With his new sun-tan glow

Man of Tweed

There is a man who suffered with dysphoria
Because he lived and grew up in an area
Where theft, drugs and drinking was rife
But he had dreams of having a better life
Including a job, a house and a loving wife

He got a job and worked very hard
Buying a car and a house with a yard
Getting married and having a dream family
Depression lifted and so got back his sanity
Living a life that once was only a fantasy

He was always obsessed with going to the gym
Making sure his body was toned, muscular and slim
It was at the gym where he met his future wife to be
Work-life balance included holidays by the sea
His heart and soul being filled with love and glee

Wearing suits to prove he was now part of the elite
Although underneath he still had the body of an athlete
With a manly strut of posture, brooding and authority
There was one thing left to achieve which was a priority
And when revealed you'll understand this parody

In his mind he genuinely believed
That in order to be perceived
As successful, rich, envied and wise
He needed to wear tweed jackets and bow ties
Despite still saying *ain't it, gob, gut and zip flies*

Maria's Daughters

You can tell they are Maria's daughters
Domesticated and sincere
Goddesses of the home
Creating food delights
Taught to them
By Maria herself

You can tell they are Maria's daughters
All of them helping whoever needs help
Offering words of wisdom
But only when needed
Being there to listen
To comfort and console

Even her daughter-in-laws
Exhibit the same traits
Kind and generous
Hard-working and content
Just like Maria's daughters
And Maria herself

You can tell they are Maria's daughters
From the warmth of their face
The generosity of their heart
Their open homes
The children they raised
Transcending the spirit of Maria

Matador

There is a woman who they call *The Matador*
Because she's fierce as the bullfighters from Ecuador
She struts around at work on the hardened floor
Treating colleagues as though her league of whores

She argues causing raised voices and severe uproar
Over mats and space and even pens, that's what for
Causing grown men and women to have heads so sore
And she's often more deadly than a forest wild boar

I'd love to send her off to Singapore
To give her family a holiday galore
But even there she'd cause a war
Becoming an aggressive dinosaur

So suck it up and pretend rapport
In order for peace at work to be restored
That is the advice that I'd implore
Or just turn around and that bitch ignore

Miniature Me (extended version)

I look at you, my son
So many things of me I see in you
Identical colour of our eyes and hair is obvious
Our skin complexion
Your smile and cheeky grin
A smirk when you know you've been naughty
When you laugh that makes me laugh just like you
The stare and look you give when hungry
You are a smaller version of myself
The miniature me

Others see our similarities
My parents notice that you sleep the way I once did
Making similar sounds that I made thirty years ago
The frown and cursing look when tired
Trying not to nod off to sleep when you are exhausted
The stare you give to us when having your nappy changed
Whilst your limbs dance in the air as though being
  electrocuted
And the manner in which you play …
Well that apparently reminds them of my toddler years
Along with your occasional tears

Yet I also see someone else in you
Your mother's curious and stunning gaze
The giggling spurts
The yawn you give

Just like the yawns she does
The slow opening and closing of your eyes when tired
But you're also developing your own nature
Like the munching of your food
The tiny grasp of your hand in ours
And the soulful adoration you give to us

You're gaining height and strength to run about
Creating your own personality
Slowly your laughter is changing too
Your walk or strut you'll make your own
In the blink of an eye you'll be making your own decisions
About your taste in food
Choosing the clothes you wear
Deciding how to style your hair
Even though you'll no longer be a miniature me
I'll still be the proudest dad there ever will be

Monday to Friday Girl

She is a creature of habit
Monday is McDonald's Day
Chicken Selects Meals
With spicy Barbeque Sauce
And Pepsi
Tuesday is KFC Day
More chicken

Wednesday is pampering day
As she visits the hair salon
You never know what look she will leave with
Hair done in a classy bun
Straightened looking like a diva
Permed like someone from the '80s
Beehive as though from the '60s
Or even a punk rocker
With pink and purple hair
Although she'll call it plum and lilac

Thursday is pizza day
But she has to have first pick
She's a very fussy eater
All her food
Has to be from a Takeaway

Friday is the nail salon
Zebra striped
Pink and Black
Blood red and silver
All to match
Whatever outfit she is wearing

Then the weekly routine starts
All over again

Morning to Mourning

Morning has broken
The EU referendum has spoken
Some people are now heartbroken
Whilst others rejoice with emotion
All over the vote that was chosen
Society no longer together or woven
A nation divided and facing erosion
Morning feels gloomy and frozen
Fading away are the years that were golden
Darkness cascades as though dawning an omen
Morning is broken
Mourning has now awoken

Mother Mourner

Her role is cemented
As the sole chief mourner
She has seen it all
Whoever dies
She will announce
That they were so close
She knew him or her best
Announcing it before they're laid to rest

Her face is withered and bleak
Wrinkled and frosty
Looking like some old hag
A wicked witch from a fairy tale
Taking delight from deaths
Disguising her spite
As genuine sadness

She will take over everything
Visiting the grieving family
Caring words given
Taking over collecting money
Choosing the sympathy card
Representing her work place colleagues
Allowing no input from anyone else

If anyone dares have an opinion
She will talk over them
Loudly and condescendingly
Ensuring that in the future

They will no longer have an opinion
As she is expert
In the field of mourning

Her funeral clothes
Hang ready in her wardrobe
For whoever dies next
Black for Christian funerals
White for Sikh funerals
Including a headscarf
Blouses, skirts, shoes, boots etc.

She practices sad looks in the mirror
Adept at causing eyes to fill with streams
As though fighting back tears
Or a look of loss
Of respect
Hiding her genuine feelings
Of glee

Winter's ice describes this woman
Frozen face crackling like broken ice
Becoming a professional ice skater
Gliding glacially amongst family and friends
Heart hardened like solid polar ice
Sub-zero soul as cold as a month of snow
Faking shivering as though in a snow storm
Her touch is arctic and sharp
As though touching a corpse in a mortuary

Negative Man

He stomps his way forward
At whirlwind speed
Like the uncouth march of a herd of buffalos
Or the weighted footprints of an adult elephant
As he spreads his poisoned perspectives
A thick dollop of lard-laced lies and exaggerations
To add merit to his forecasts of doom and gloom

Puffs of hot air accompany his words of woe
Like a bow against the strings of a violin
Although a trumpet is probably a more apt metaphor
As he bellows out his acidic prophecies
Not to mention stories about other people
Excitement on his face as he comments on their
  misfortunes
It isn't fresh air that he breathes into his mouth and nostrils
But gossip, hatred and curses bestowed on chosen foes

Plump cheeks with a healthy glow of red
Probably brought on through high blood pressure
As it is rumours and condemnation that runs through his
  veins
He sees negative traits in everyone he knows or sees
Positive comments are alien to him
And if he hears a positive comment he shoots them down
With his unique brand of negative bullets

He has a fortunate and blessed life
Even though his intelligence is limited

Compassion for other human beings is non-existent
Yet he expects that others should feel sorrow for him
Unaware that they do indeed feel pity of another kind
The kind that is accompanied by shudders in their spine
Cringing with embarrassment and disgust
As they tolerate the sad pathetic lonely negative man

Obsession

She wants exclusivity with him
Volcano emotions erupting
When she sees him with other women
Her temper flares
Hotter than the sun
Rationality disappears
As demands she makes
Are unreasonable and shocking
Virtually steering him
Towards other women

He wants to be helpful
Oblivious to his charms
The manner in which women
Compete for his attention
Demanding his time
Through manipulative ways
Excuses to touch his back or hand
To laugh loudly in an enticing manner
Making her body as sexy as possible
Alluring, amorous and available

The attention he receives
Is pleasurable and entertaining
Despite his love and sexual prowess
Being reserved solely for his wife
The women who chase after him
Are encased in a snow globe
But the weather inside is heated
From frustration, anger and desire
As they imagine being with him
Obsession manifesting into hate

Poison

She creates potent potions
Weasels her way into families
As though she was always there
She mixes her concoctions
Dissolving her way into their blood

She knows who to target
Those who are vulnerable
Who are lonely or need help
She smiles so sweetly and innocently
Whilst poisoning them

Someone who has care needs
She will lessen the burden to herself
As the potion will make them drowsy
Sleeping their way through the day
Whilst she takes what she wants

To those who are bereft of love
She'll become their lover
Adding toxic spices to meals and cups of tea
Ensuring they are susceptible to her suggestions
Before again taking everything she wants

She is pure poison
Quickly disappearing
After lives have been destroyed
Already having worked her way
Into the lives of her next victims

Poster Boy

They call him the *Poster Boy*
Not because he has the looks
To model Versace products
Hugo Boss, or Armani

Instead he has the ideal image
To be a *Poster Boy*
For the products he uses
McDonald's, KFC and Pizza Hut

Pride

According to Aristotle pride is a virtue
Whereas some religions say that pride
Is one of the seven deadly sins
Along with greed, lust, malicious envy,
Gluttony, wrath and sloth

A man who is truly full of pride
Will be proud of all his accomplishments;
Career, Home Life, Wealth, Possessions, and Health
Walking as though high and mighty
Looking over and protecting his own pride
Becoming virtuous and a worthy King of lions

Procrastinator

There is a guy I know
Who is extremely slow
At getting things done
Yet daily he has a run
After going to the gym
In order to be fit and slim

He is full of good intentions
But ends up with procrastinations
Because there's too much to do
And in his head there is a queue
He says he will do this and that
But his actions invariably fall flat

There is always an excuse
And eventually you deduce
That he'll never follow through
Despite best intentions wanting to
He is basically the ultimate creator
Of being an extreme procrastinator

Punctuation

She used to be a headmistress
At a nursery school
And primary school
Even though, that was many years ago
She still reads
With her face rising in colour
Rivalling a beautiful red rose
As she notices mistakes
Commenting on poems
How there's no full stops
No commas or other grammar
And in her mind
Over and over
Is one word

Punctuate, PUNCTUATE, PUNCTUATE

Puppet

You cannot see the strings
Invisible to the eyes
But they are there
Moving those around him
To dance to his tune

He is in their mind
Fingers flowing up and down
Brains being played like a piano
All decisions appearing to be
Independent

When things fall apart
You will be there alone
Taking in all the responsibility
Your psyche and soul burning
Life turning into ash

The puppet master will not care
For he has many others to control
To play with as though toy dolls and soldiers
Smiling as he destroys lives with no remorse
Adding more and more puppets to his collection

Reach

His reach is far and wide
Not confined to where his hands grab
Heavy and clasping over beautiful bodies
As he undresses them
With the uncouthness of his personality
Entering into their intimacy
Selfishly satisfying his desires
A disgusting addiction
Inflicted onto pitiful souls
Which he has now destroyed

His reach is far and wide
That mouth which slobbers over hers
And in other places too
Her nude body has become like plasticine
For him to mould her as he pleases
The mouth which he also uses to issue threats
Which he has the ability to carry out
Because his reach is far and wide

The smell and touch of him
Lingers forever in their minds
Along with the tone of his threats
Even with therapy they cannot escape
He remains like an echo made of steel
Unbreakable
All because of his reach
Which continues to be far and wide

He believes that he is charismatic
That his wealth makes him untouchable
Like an omnipotent Olympian God
Who also satisfied their lusts with mortal women
Then discarded them as damaged and unclean
A prostitute gives her body willingly
Receiving her payment as agreed
But these women are treated like a herd of animals
Or like the muddy fields where those animals trample on

If they do disobey his commands
And reveal what he has done
He carries out the threats he made
Continuing making them his victim
Disparaging their honesty
Giving them a brand new image
Of being conniving, greedy liars
Because he has power
And his reach is far and wide

Resisting Harassment

He gives you compliments galore
Talented in striking up a rapport
You soak them up, wanting more
As though clamouring for an encore
His flattering words, you do adore

Comments change into what you deplore
Sexual overtures that you cannot ignore
Saying that he wants you to be his whore
That your body will become his to explore
Until he makes you feel dirty, tired and sore

Those wicked words you do abhor
Making your blood boil and soar
You tell him to back off with a roar
He issues threats that rip you to the core
Crushing your spirit which you cannot restore

Rewarded

Aggressively she verbally attacks
Almost everyone she meets
Using her height and coarse voice
Looking like an old crone
Bullying people is what she likes to do
Then accuses the bullied person
Of being the bully

She has two henchwomen
Together they look like a coven of witches
Cackling away as they torment colleagues
Bellowing out as they force managers
To dance to their tune
The trembling, shaking dance of fear
And of being terrorised and threatened

Yet through all their machinations
Through the tactics that they have perfected
They get rewarded with secret promotions
To get more money and influence
Whilst their real reward is kept secret from them
As their lonely, ear-bashed and unfulfilled husbands
Seek and find fulfilment elsewhere

Routine

There is a man who's exceptionally keen
To make sure that his body is muscular and lean
Daily at 6.00 am to the gym he does convene
Uses bench press, push ups, crunches and the treadmill
  machine
Pumping up his testosterone and adrenaline
In order to make his body fit, sturdy and serene

After the gym he takes care of his hygiene
A shower to make sure that he is clean
And products he uses to make himself preen
Even on his lips he puts on Vaseline
All part of his usual routine
In order not to smell of body sweat and odour that's
  unclean

His food he examines to maximise protein
But doesn't particularly enjoy veg that is green
He knows about the added energy of caffeine
Frequently buys and chomps on chocolate from the works
  canteen
This is what makes up his entire cuisine
So don't be alarmed if he frequently visits the latrine

Now the time has come to start to be mean
About the man who forgets he is no longer nineteen
Could it be that in his nature he is really libertine?
Dreaming of fame and being driven in a limousine
But what natural skills could he glean?
To give him more wealth than England's Queen

Perhaps to become an actor appearing on a movie screen?
Or as a model in a famous magazine
Advertising swimwear and sunscreen
The future is always unforeseen
If offered enough money would he allow himself to be
  between …
Two staples as a nude centrefold with a pose that is
  obscene?

Rugby

Hooligan chants and grunts
Whilst wearing solidarity uniform
Adrenaline rush
Blood pressure rising
Power of the scrum
Running with feet splattering the field
Inhaling and exhaling the cold fresh air
Electric charged veins and speed
Muscles taut, strong and fully utilised
Throwing the oval leathered ball
Spinning through the air
Catch and run
Elbow and shoulder thumps
Bruises and cuts received with pride
Which merge with the dirt on the skin
Touchdown successes
Smiles and frowns
Of winners and losers
The exhilarating sport;
Women's Rugby League

Selfie-Dude

There is a type of man called selfie-dude
Who take photos of themselves that are lewd
They enjoy posing a stance that is rude
And even selfies of themselves in the nude

They take photos that make you leer
Because they pose without fear
With everything on display to appear
Including their naked rear

On social media the photos are viewed
With numerous clicks on *thumbs up* in gratitude
Watching that dude being quite crude
Except for those that are a bit of a prude

Now what more is there that we can say?
About these men with everything on display
Except that they are creative in the way
That they portray themselves as risqué

Seriously

A stubborn woman
Who is often cheeky
Knowing how to get her own way
Throwing the occasional
Temper tantrum
Or sulking as though wounded
Sometimes begging
Other times shouting
Even swearing
But the most frequently used technique
Is using one word
With a high-pitched tone of amazement
Both in her voice and face
"Seriously?"

Sexy Man

I get out of bed
All ruffled and hot
Muscles still tense
From being utilised the previous night
Stepping into the shower
I start to scrub my physique
Saturated in shower gel foam and aromas
Beginning to awaken
Alert and psyched

With a towel around my waist
I comb and wax my hair
Each strand to precision
The blade swipes away the facial stubble
Spraying on aftershave
Increasing confidence
Brushing my teeth
Minty fresh breath
Looking in the mirror and being impressed

I button up my white shirt
Tuck it into the suit trousers
Buckle up the belt
Put on my tie
Tug my collar in front of that mirror
Before wearing the jacket
Tugging at its lapels
Whilst adoring my reflection

No matter what I wear
Suited up, or jeans and a t-shirt
I make sure that I look handsome and stunning
Even in the nude
I am the epitome of masculinity
I might not be sophisticated to Mensa levels
Knowing all about how chemicals work
But I am expert
In human chemistry, biology and physiology

Everywhere I go
Women gather round
Competing for attention
They laugh and chit-chat
Tilting their heads and smiling
Showing off their sexiness
Enticing and available
Our words are suggestive, alluring and provocative
All expert in the competitive art of seduction

Men want to be my friend
They flock like obedient sheep
Trying to learn how I do it
Listening to my stories
Of which there are many
Siphoning off how to behave
Imitating even my strut walk
Using words that I recognise
As their order is what I created

I look after my torso
By going to the gym

Perfecting each aspect
With a muscular framed body
Rippled and ripped
Frequently visited and explored
By various hands
Masterfully pleasuring each other
Reaching heightened levels of satisfaction

A glint in my eyes
No need to be on the prowl
To be intoxicated
Or pumped up with narcotic stimulants
Everything about me is natural
A personality that's cool
Humbly and humorously accepting
All that life has to offer
Thrilling and sexy to the extreme

Sexy Woman

Where ever I go male heads turn to my direction
Women scowl and frown
The men flock to where I am
Competing for attention
Whilst the women continue steaming
Holding firm their internal silent screaming
The heat in the room escalates
Increased testosterone and adrenaline
Pitted against female hormones and pheromones
All in the shadow of my sexiness

The men continue in their chit-chat
Trying to out-do each other
Focused on expressing their strengths
Their personality they lay on a platter
Trying to impress and egress
Talents they throw into the mix
Muscles they flex
Offers are made
They make their intentions progress
Through finesse and verbal excess

The women comment and gossip
Astounded at why they are being ignored
What possible magic do I posses
I don't have any more money than them
They try to attract the men back
But the hive are mesmerised by my honey
Oblivious to the tensions they are causing

The jealousy that they are creating
All because they want to seduce me
The sexy woman in the room

My appeal is no secret, ladies
It is in the genuineness of my smile
The glint and sparkle in my eyes
It's in the curve of my shoulders
The smell of my perfume
It's in the elegance of my head held high and proud
My listening ears
So that I know just what to say
It is in the giggles and the laughter
In the humour and the repartee

Yet you're still looking mystified
On how those men to me seem hypnotised
It's in my facial expressions
It is in the legs that are ladders to the heavens
In the clothes that I wear
Not caring how on others it might compare
No need to rely on make-up to embellish and enhance
It's in my low-toned husky voice
But not like a siren of the sea
Drawing men to their deathly doom

Are you beginning to understand now why men are
riveted?
It's in my personality
My character
The essence of my life
I'm spirited

Cheekily telling them all the truth
No criticism or judgement
Or raising of my voice
A glass is the only thing I'll raise
It is in the sexiness of me

Shattered Lives

Known for his confidence
Thirsty for his next conquest
Oozing charisma
He utilises techniques at his command
The ultimate predator of women

They believe his words
And succumb to his endeavours
Sexually satisfied
Then disregarded
As he moves onto the next victim

The wife knows he is addicted
She's given up on claiming exclusive rights
Focuses her life on their children
With a plastered smile upon her face
To conceal her internal pain

The regular mistress demands more time
Followed by extra entitlements
She secures authority into his life
Due to knowing many of his secrets
And leaches off his money

At work he uses his position
To seduce women
Both the young and middle aged
They are captivated by his attention
Then yield to amorous temptation

He spends time with his children
Together they play and laugh
It's a pleasure of a different kind
Will they turn out like their father?
Or will they see the hurt their mother hides?

A bottle falls and shatters on the floor
The shards of broken glass
Representing the forgotten women
Ghostly figures from your past
You are a veteran of vice

Shoe-Stealing Sisters

They don't look at all alike
They are both thin
But the one looks
Like she's been starved of food
Whereas the other one
Wears thick Deidre Barlow glasses
Or should that be Deidre Rachid
Or maybe Deidre Hunt or Deidre Langton
If you're old enough to remember those names

They have four years between them
Throughout their teenage years
They managed to share clothes and shoes
Forcing their different sized feet
Into each other's shoes
Each sister encouraging the other
To buy the shoes that she really wants to wear
Which they then steal from each other

It's almost as though they are
Cinderella's ugly step sisters
As they cramp their feet into shoes that don't fit
Not that they are ugly
Or even living a Fairy Tale life
There is no Prince Charming
That visits where they live
Or a Fairy Godmother with a magic wand

Fast forward twenty-five years
The mothers are now encouraging their own daughters
Which clothes and shoes to buy
A trick they learnt in their youth
And when those daughters
Can't find those expensive clothes and shoes
They look into their mother's wardrobe
Which enters into another world
Like the Lion, the witch and the wardrobe
Only this one is full of shoes

Snake in a Suit

He has a grandfatherly face
With a smile that radiates warmth
Speaking in a dignified manner
Self-assured and confidant

His smooth mannerisms
Makes you reveal all
Giving him the ammunition
That he seeks

You won't realise
That he is the one responsible
For your misfortunes and misery
As he embeds jagged sharp swords
Again and again into your back

That is where his smile comes from
Enjoying ripping people's lives apart
Ruthless and vindictive
Revelling that nothing will come back to him
As he is expert in his trade

He doesn't flinch when lying
His façade is woven into his DNA
Slimy, slick, shady, sly and serpentine
Nothing more than a snake in a suit

Stubborn Woman

She's off on one again
A stern and scolding face
Like concrete setting under the furnace sun
Scorched layer on top of the usual ashen complexion

Harsher than a magistrate with a 100% conviction rate
Never able to find anyone innocent
Locating words that were never spoken
Implied, innuendo and insistent
Fierce and ferocious in her attack

The person on the receiving end
Is aggravated and antagonised to the extreme
Forced to defend themselves
But continually ridiculed by the stubborn woman

Those in attendance shy away from becoming involved
Obedient jury members instructed to convict
Despite knowing that the accused is innocent
Because all are afraid to challenge the stubborn woman
In case they become her next victim

Sympathy

There are people who want your sympathy
They crave it and are skilful in their techniques
Pretending that their issues are a genuine crisis
Fluttering their eyes as though fighting the tears
Draining the energy of those under their spell
Whilst being absolved of their huge ineptness
Caused by their immense laziness
Progressing in life with tenacious leeching
Trampling and rude to those who are expendable
Envious of people who have progressed
Wanting their position and power

The sympathy seeker
Believes that they are able to fool everyone
That they deserve wealth and luxury
Solace and sorrow
When what they really need
Is empathy and truth
That others have suffered in life
Who are brave and accepting
To be shown a better way of living
Achieving through hard work
Appreciating the value of others
Instead of continually striving for sympathy

Tamed

He is fuelled by arrogance and anger
An uncontrollable raging fire
Flames burning those around him
Scorching and even reducing them to ash

No one is safe
He doesn't have respect for anyone
Everyone who comes into contact with him
Will sooner or later be a selected victim

Even those who have authority
Are scared and sometimes petrified
As he will combat them with bellowing fury
His wrath alien to human compassion or emotions

Until a woman he desires comes along
She is his match and superior in every way
Behind the scenes she scolds and tames the evil man
Amazing everyone that wild animals can be tamed

Temperamental Father

There is no denying
That this man is temperamental
He walks in a rush
As though the wind ushers him along
His face is stern and authoritative
Wearing wrinkles of arguments galore
Arguments fuelled with anger and fire
With stinging venom and brimstone

He loves money
Eyes lighting up like scorching flames of the sun
Feeling the notes beneath his fingers
Is more amorous than the feel of smooth skin
He flicks his fingers over the notes as he counts
More sensuous than fingers gliding over a naked body
Coins are amassed on the table like a hundred Rapunzel's
towers
He breathes in the money as though oxygen for survival

He adores his self-acclaimed image as a man of charity
Quickly creating charitable events
Glaring at people to donate
Vocal about his organisational skills
Gloating about all the good deeds he has done
He has aided charities all over the world
Truly a saintly figure amongst mortals
Silent about his cut from the donations

There is no denying
That this man truly believes
That his word should be obeyed
That there should be no questions
No explanations given
For he the law of the land
The voice of God on Earth
For he is a Priest

Temptation

Imagine what you would do
You are a happily married man
You love your wife and your children
Another sexy woman wants you
She makes herself available to you
Promising that no one will ever know
She'll do whatever you want her to do
Sends you alluring photos of herself
In all kinds of provocative stances
Especially of herself in the nude
What will you choose to do?

Temptress

Married men are more appealing to her
Especially the ones that are happily married
They're the ones that she finds challenging
She uses a multitude of techniques
To capture them in her snare

Promises that no one will ever find out
Saturating them in compliments and adulation
Being teasing, provocative and suggestive
Or becoming sulky and demonstratively demanding
Not to mention the photos that she sends

The temptress is willing to become whatever you want
Do whatever you want, and whenever you want it done
Morals are no obstacle and she doesn't believe in them
She's there in her availability to you
Have you decided what you will do?

That Man

There is a man whose heart is like a stone
Hard and heavy
Impenetrable and icy cold
His soul is without light
Living and thriving in total darkness
Revelling in his demonic traits

There are many things which he does love
Much more than his wife and children
Power and ambition
Making more money than others he knows
Demeaning virtually all those around him
Whilst offering false platitudes to those he thinks can
further his societal standing

Devious and cunning
Convincing in his lies
Ruins lives with delight
Honours himself as superior
Arrogance rises
With the ferocity of volcanic lava

He thinks that he is admired
That people are envious of his good fortune
Of his position, possessions and even looks
Oblivious that he is pitied
Disrespected and hated
That man who is devoid of humanity

That Woman

She smiles
The heavens themselves awaken
Her fingers whisk through her hair
Adding to the high levels of chemistry floating in the air
Those delicate fingers then slowly caresses her neck
She knows the art of seduction
It is her domain

Did she wink?
Those beautiful eyes are wide and alive
Dark and mysterious
They are beckoning me towards her
Silent eyes
But as alluring as the singing of a siren
And perhaps just as deathly

The back of her right hand strokes down her left arm
Slowly
Making sure that I observe her entire body
Her black dress so tight against her physique
Slender and toned
Oozing sex appeal
And she knows it

Those legs
Smooth and well defined
With her heel locked to the floor
Tapping away a melodious tune
A secret Morse code to draw men towards her
Selectively choosing the hunkiest and most fit
Seducing them to a night of sexual fulfilment

Those Were the Times

At work you spent so many hours
Ensuring all your work got done;
Calculating budgets and quality results
Assessing performance reviews and analysing data
Allocating work and dealing with grievances
Making sure everyone else did their work

People gave you grief
Tempers could flare
And then subside
Words exchanged could be unpleasant;
Honest and brutal, or even cruel
Occasionally, words of kindness and humour

When people were having tough times
You were there
Not judging
Talking and guiding
Available
Advice and action given

Hard decisions you made
Results then followed
A testament to your decision making
Looking back
Yes, there were difficult times
But in the end, you achieved and did succeed

Tight Shirt

Your shirt's too tight
It doesn't look right
You think you look cool
But just look like a tool

You're wrong, so very wrong
They show my guns are strong
Making women salivate and drool
As if I am their man-prized jewel

They continue in their verbal duel
As she says, you're such a fool
That shirt looks like you've had it since pre-school
She smiles a smile that's oh so cruel

But before he can say another word
She continues making herself heard
You need to buy shirts that fit
Instead of ones that look like they're gonna split

They continue with their repartee
Trying to outwit each other with glee
Flirtatious comments to strike bingo
The bimbo and the himbo

Time to Write

Have you heard about the group, *Time to Write?*
What they write they should be feeling contrite
Ursula writes on paper, perhaps she's a Luddite?
Angela writes about angels who actually fight
And a teenager who tries to kill herself alright
But ends up being saved from the death light

Janet writes about gardens suffering from frostbite
The wife who killed her husband by candlelight
A Birmingham floozie in a jacuzzi under moonlight
Ann relives her life's current strife and highlights
Published author is David who will give you insight
Just do not criticise him because he will backbite

Martin has followed David's footsteps and become a
  playwright
Sending people he knows a *Spoke – In The Lamp* invite
Where stand-up poets, including himself, are under the
  limelight
Mario writes complete rubbish and filthy shite
About randy men and women of the night
Work related tales of horror and hateful spite

That *Time to Write group* every month do unite
They remember Samantha who was so bright
They then take it in turn to be under the spotlight
As their own work they then each begin to recite
Looking at them you'd think they were so polite
But I must admit, listening to them is a secret delight

Too Late

You are intelligent
Yet you are oblivious
To how that man
Managed to control you

An invisible parasite
Attached to your brain
Only this animal
Is destroying your independence

You continue to believe
That decisions made are your own
Unaware that you are doing
Exactly what he wants you to do

You are happy and content with life
Joyous and happy-go-lucky
Oblivious that you are no longer you
Merely an echo of him

The tone of your voice
Is still beautiful and crisp
Which disguises his words that you use
Which others begin to realise

Unfortunately, it will be too late
For once you realise the truth
The damage will have been done
Wrecked lives and even livelihoods

Transformation into a Metrosexual Man

Determined to transform his body
Which he thinks is fat and shoddy
To the gym he goes day after day
On the scales himself he does weigh
Protein shakes he begins to drink
Healthy food he eats which does stink
Along with fat burners to help him along
Determined to eventually look good in a thong

The fat finally begins to burn
Muscles he now starts to yearn
Increasing the time he spends at the gym
In order to become slim and trim
He hits the weight lifting hard
Alcohol he temporarily does discard
Along with the junk food he used to eat
Slowly becoming a muscled athlete

Next he attacks the hair on his chest
In order to look good when undressed
To the waxing and tanning salon he goes
When he leaves he has a suntan that glows
He buys products to preen himself
So that he never ends up on the shelf
There are those that think he'll eventually quit
Until they see the selfies which show he's now fit

Webbed Life

Invisible threads spin out of her life
As intricate as a spider's web
Luring men into her lair
Walking seductively on flimsy silk lines
To reach her intended prey

So many fibres from which to choose
Each leading to a different man
Her men
All of them
Hers

And not just leading to different men
But the varied locations
Secret rendezvous
Lurid affairs
Satisfying her thirst and hunger

Quite in contrast to the tapestry of Penelope
The faithful Queen of Odysseus
Simple lives in ancient Ithaca
Goat herders in mountains
Waiting for their King to return

Whilst back to the modern woman
Weaving her own web
Faster than Arachne of Greek Myth
Always tempestuous
And naturally discreet

A wink and a smile
More beautiful than a Goddess
They're captivated by her beauty
She's won one more heart
The woman and her spinning web

Then late at night she does return
Entering her home as silently as she can
Not to disturb anyone there
Quieter than a spider waiting on the edge of her web
Whilst her husband continues his snoring

When Egotists Collide

They both enjoy and revel in bullying
Two tall men with bellowing voices
Humiliating people until totally annihilated
Driving some to madness and paranoia
Others becoming desperate, desolate and depressed
Even committing suicide or downward spiral to death
They have much more in common than just that
They chase women for entertainment
Suggestive in what they can do for each other
The women succumb to their sexual advances
Allowing their body and soul to be demeaned
Hard-core acts of warped minds
Becoming mere meat to be devoured
By savages
Promised jobs or promotions disappear
Disregarding once the lusts of the power hungry egotists
Have been satisfied

Eventually they do collide
Over women or power
Or sometimes both
For the egotist sees everything as a war
Which they have to win
Clashing like two supervillains
Both using the tools that have served them well
Lies, trickery, and more lies
Equally matched in deviousness
In being totally unrelenting
Two adult lions clashing

To take charge of the pride
Teeth gnawing at flesh
Determined to take down their rival
Those who are in awe of the egotists
Take sides or sulk away as though oblivious
The rest watch and enjoy the show

Wicked Woman

She's vicious and vindictive
Spreading rumours, gossip and slander
Creating myths
Demonising those she does not like
Which is more or less everyone she meets

Each time you think
That she cannot get any lower
With her wicked words
And treacherous tongue
She surprises you once more

Even the death of a loved one
Cannot dilute her wickedness
As she crushes reputations
Determined to show that she knows best
Unaware that she is being disrespectful

Wicked Words

They attack the elements and essence of my soul
Determined to have me in bits rather than whole
With words designed to annihilate me and cajole
But despite their vicious efforts I am still in control
Allowing their continued shameful verbal stroll
Ignorant that they're digging their own solitary hole

He's fat, she's smelly, he's got no friends
Look at those zits! He needs some cleanse
Your words could result in their life's ends
And then it'll be too late to make amends
Just because your parents own Mercedes Benz
Does not mean your life is worth more dividends

Do you know what struggles they have gone through?
My guess is that you probably do not have a clue
Yet wicked words you spread as though all true
But think about if the tables were turned on you
Your character, personality and looks they devalue
Because sometimes in life we get what we are due

Wolverhampton's Witch

There is a witch that lives in Wolverhampton
She's got long black hair like the witches of old
But is modern as she goes to the gym every day
Watching the calories that she eats
Determined to become super spiny and slim

There is a witch that lives in Wolverhampton
She's got crooked teeth like the witches of old
Able to look busy when really just lazy and fake
Pretending to be friendly whilst actually deceptive
Money hungry and hypnotised by bling

There is a witch that lives in Wolverhampton
She's got jealousy traits like the witches of old
Tries to talk posh even though she's not
Hides the facial blotches and hairy warts
Through makeup and magical potions

There is a witch that lives in Wolverhampton
Her cauldron is hidden like the witches of old
In her home where she lives with her husband
Living a contemporary life
Driving a car instead of using her broomstick

There is a witch that lives in Wolverhampton
Feigning to be normal like the witches of old
Even though she's conniving and bitchy
Plotting her success and the misery of others
Just like those ancient dark souled witches of old

Woman from Pelsall

There is a young woman from Pelsall
She collects perfume bottles galore
Displays them as part of her home's décor
There's enough to open her own shop or stall

With a pen she begins to scrawl
Stories that do entertain and enthral
The last line reveals what does befall
The hero or heroine's downfall

A story of a woman who wore a shawl
Hiding the dagger that she used to maul
Her enemy in the heart, the neck and eye ball
Stories that make you frightened, gasp and gall

There is something she told me I do recall
The revelation will alarm you and appal
Those perfume bottles are full of ethanol
Her murderous stories aren't made up at all

Womaniser

He struts around at work
With a smile that's a smirk
He sees women as his perk
But he's really a middle aged jerk

There are women who do succumb
As he uses his management income
To supply the booze for her to become
His latest sexual lay of girls so dumb

Then to his wife he does return
Inside she's full of infernal burn
His addiction she cannot overturn
And learns to hide away her discern

If your adult children turn out like you?
Behaving randy through and through
Despite being married, lovers they accrue
Will your life you begin to review?

Many years from now, will your kids forgive
The manner in which your life you did live
And given the chance would you re-live
A life with no conquests, you'd willingly omit

Words

You're spreading words again that are unkind
Designed to break my spirit and my mind
You think that I am oblivious and blind
That my reputation you malign and grind
With wicked words I cannot escape or leave behind
But I have inner belief and strength that I will find

Those lying words gather speed like a raging fire
Dangerous like invisible deathly daggers that are dire
They stab at me again and again; the words of the liar
But you will not gain what you desire or aspire
For me to become desolate, depressed and perspire
Your words and lies I can defuse and even satire

The words that you continue to utter are full of disdain
Without reason or merit you continue to try to inflict pain
Your obsession has become as addictive as cocaine
As savage as a wild beast you have become inhumane
Those evil and malignant words are ultimately in vain
Because despite your all efforts my sanity I still retain

The energy used in the rumours that you construe
To try to encase me into a suffocating mood of blue
And to annihilate my character through and through
Is saddening and pathetic, but you are unable to view
The realistic reputation that you yourself accrue
As people begin to realise words spoken are untrue

Is there a reason why you use such hateful words to hurt
  me?
Once spoken those powerful words will expand and flow
  free
Like an acorn that grows and grows into an oak tree
Do you want those words to drown my spirit as if beneath
  the sea?
Are you so weak that such gossiping words can cause you
  to glee?
Well those words have failed to cripple me, and that I
  guarantee

Words of a Cocky Adulterer

To the mistress
He brags about himself
Makes all kinds of offers
To seduce her
Make her do the dirty things he likes
Tells her that he loves her
Explains his wife doesn't understand him
Or how horrible his wife is
That the wife can't get hurt if she doesn't know
Surely they deserve to be happy
Proven words which he's used on other women
Continuing his efforts until he gets what he wants

To his friends
He also brags about himself
About the women that he's had
That he's so lucky
Having a wife and a mistress
Laughing about his exploits
The positions that they've tried
Making bets on other women
Whether she will succumb to his charms
And how long it will take
Enjoys rating his conquests
Shameless in all his conversations

To his wife
He carries on as though they are happy
Tells her what she wants to hear

Reacts offended if accused of adultery
Tries to make the wife feel guilty
His lies and excuses are already prepared
Mates are also used for his cover-up stories
In the event of overwhelming evidence
More lies come trickling out
That his wife is the one he really loves
Cliché remarks that have been uttered by others before
She doesn't mean anything to me

To himself
He justifies all of his actions
Believes he deserves to have both a wife and a mistress
His desires need to be satisfied
Truly believing that his mates who know
Are envious of him
That his wife should live in ignorance
Or accept his adulteress ways
Greedy and cheeky
Arrogant, confident, egotistical and vain
Living a dangerous life
Living only in the moment

Work Wars

You do not have to look far
To find a feud, battle or war
Often gruesome and venomous
On-going arguments
Machinations and calculations
Getting vengeance
Threats and spiteful insults

There are wars to rise the ranks
Rivalries of work, love and lust
Automatic relationships of hate
Loathing and repulsive glares
Fear and intimidation
False friendships
Gaining your trust
Before ripping you apart
Starting with your innocent heart

Cliques focusing on isolated individuals
Like packs of wolves on prey
Often due to jealously and envy
There are those that are flirting
Whilst others are in despair and hurting
Some colleagues are working
But many are work shy and shirking

Hurling poisoned remarks
Like the wicked witch
Offering an apple laced with poison

Spreading rumours and innuendo
As easily as butter melting in a pan
Becoming too hot to handle
Eventually burning out of control
Singeing everything around

Work wars
Lasting days, months or even years
Managers, staff and colleagues
Who are either victorious, or shamed and destroyed
Driven and damned to despair, desolation and depression
Becoming victims who might as well be corpses
Unless of course they rise
Courageously fighting back
Determined not to loose
And so the battles and wars of work
Thrive and continue

Write to Right

Many years ago someone said to me that I was unable to
write
Those words he delivered with deliberate and malicious
spite
He clearly wanted me to enter a competition to viciously
backbite
But I did not respond to his goading or feed his cancerous
appetite
His smile was wide and teeth were gleaming, revelling in
delight
Thinking that my spirit and strength he had managed to
blight
And all I could think was, you really shouldn't smile in
sunlight
Crooked teeth. Smell of eggs. Enough to make you vomit
alright

Something internally his embittered words they did stir and
ignite
They gave me determination, courage and renewed inner
might
I started typing away on the desktop both during the day
and night
Skills I developed and conquered giving me a totally new
insight
At times I'd want to cry. I'd smile. I've even laughed with
excite
Words spoken intending to cause me to feel low and in a
plight
Have actually given me a living and that's surely pure
dynamite
The odour and teeth of the bad man, well they're still just
not right

Yesterday's News

It's major news
Hot topics of the day
An illicit affair
A suspension
An accusation
A fight
A criminal offence

You feel their pain
Their anguish
You want to offer them support
Whilst others fuel the gossip
Speculation and rumours
The best and the worst
Of human attitudes

The emotions are intense
Explosive and debilitating
Yet within days
Sometime even hours
Your disgraced name has disappeared
New victims are dissected and discussed
And you are just yesterday's news

Your Management Team

Mr. Smith, will you remember your management team?
Who started off as a nightmare, rather than a dream
You had to be firm and words exchanged were extreme
But when needed, you would encourage their self esteem

At times those managers made you almost scream
However, almost as though a magical trick or scheme
They found increased strength and targets they'd redeem
And so those managers finally began to achieve and gleam

To summarise your management team under your regime
Became number one in the country and so reigned supreme
You became the cat that found its beloved whipped cream
And as you leave, their invisible hidden tears will stream

More Poetry Books from Mario

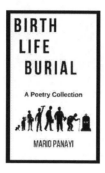

This is a poetry book concerning birth, life and death and all the ups and downs our unique adventure brings. There are over 100 poems written in a variety of voices and moods. Poems which are endearing and emotive, some that are humorous and comedic, and others which are thought provoking. Spanning a number of topics including childhood, love, parenthood, betrayal, older age, suicide, and death, these memorable and refreshing poems are varied in form (such as rhyme and free verse) and also in length.

There is also a number of allegory poems. The various poems are presented from different perspectives, such as from the parent or the child, the person proposing, the person being cheated upon, and from an independent/third party point of view. Whatever stage of life you may have reached, you will have experienced some of the emotions or events shared in Birth, Life, Burial.

Buy your copy here: https://amzn.to/31oafSt

This is a poetry book concerning myths, legends, fairy tales, and other make-believe characters and fictional entities. There are over 100 poems. Examples of Greek Myth characters includes Zeus and Hera, Atlas, Medusa and the Gorgon sisters, Python, Arachne, the Minotaur and the Labyrinth, the Sphynx, the Kraken, and many more.

There is Audhumbla from Norse mythology. From the Old Testament there are poems about Noah, Lot's wife, Cain from Cain and Able, Lilith, David and Goliath, Salome, Angels, and the Devil. Poems about Legends includes King Arthur, Excalibur, and the Lady of the Lake. There are also poems about Dragons, Fairy Tales, Easter Island, Witches, Black Cats, Monsters, Clowns, Ghosts, Werewolves, and the Tooth Fairy. Finally, there are also poems about places such as Ireland, Prague, Cannock Chase, and castles.

The poems are in a variety of voices, and different moods such as serious, thought-provoking and emotive, or humorous and comedic.

Buy your copy here: https://amzn.to/2VPyLef

About the Author

Mario Panayi was born in the UK, but visited his relatives in Cyprus every year during his childhood. It was a very different Cyprus in the 1970s and early 1980s compared to now as Cyprus had been invaded in 1974. The visits he made to Cyprus were very influential on Mario, as he witnessed the aftermath of war such as refugees living in tiny accommodation, running water half a day per week which had to be stored for the whole week, no telephones, and of course more than 2,000 people had disappeared, presumed dead. This included two of his cousins.

It made Mario very conscious of how fortunate most people are in life, including himself, and how precious life is. He also forged a close relationship to his relatives in Cyprus. Mario found that being told he couldn't do things just made him more determined to be able to do things. At school a teacher refused to sign off his university application, explaining that there was no point applying to University because he was not capable academically of getting a degree and would probably not be accepted at University. He applied regardless and got two honours degrees, one postgraduate degree and two Masters degrees, including an MBA.

At a previous job he was told by his manager that he could not write. It was at that point he went on to get his final degree which was a BA (HONS) Philosophy and Creative and Professional Writing, but he never studied poetry.

Mario has found that walking and writing is cathartic and therapeutic.

To date he has published three poetry books:

- *Birth, Life, Burial* (2018)
- *Myths and Make-Believe* (2018)
- *Do You Recognise Yourself* (2019)

Made in the USA
Lexington, KY
07 December 2019